The Golden Rule for Le

The Second Most Powerful Principle in the Universe

Printed in the United States of America

ISBN 978-0-6151-8647-4

Cover and book design by Jeff Rossignol

Acknowledgements

I cannot express enough my debt to mentors. When I consider the role of a father and the expression of self-sacrifice for the wellbeing of another, I am compelled to express overwhelming and humble gratitude for the "fathers" God has placed in my life.

From Maine to Pennsylvania to West Virginia God has strategically sent fathers to watch over me and give me guidance. These men have shared their lives and experiences with me. These fathers shared not from pride but with a loving and caring heart to help me accomplish my destiny. Their expression of fatherhood is truly The Golden Rule in its purest form.

Vincent Rossignol, Christopher Cote, Robert Smock, Douglas Shrier, Jim Embrey. Thank you for giving of your life and your love for the well-being of others. I always weigh your words heavily upon my heart. The journey is far from over and your guidance and love is valued more than the greatest treasures. This book is a shallow reflection of the wisdom you have poured onto me. It is my hope to emulate the model you have provided to those God places in my care.

Your Son

The Golden Rule for Leaders

The Second Most Powerful Principle in the Universe

Table of Contents

INTRODUCTION

If you have this information in your possession, you have arrived at the beginning of new opportunities. Contained within this book is the most profound truth that will revolutionize your business.

I guarantee that the more you understand and apply this truth to your organization the greater the unity, ownership, productivity, and profitability you and your organization will experience. This is the second most important principle in the entire world for you to know! Focus all your energy and efforts into applying this principle correctly. As a leader, the CAP (correctly applied principle) of the second most powerful principle must be your highest goal. Everything else you do hang in the balance of this principle.

Before I actually tell you what the principle is I want to challenge you to listen carefully to its characteristics and benefits. The reason for this is that you should be willing to listen with an unbiased and open mind. The challenge of the most powerful and profound truths in the world is that they seem neither powerful nor profound. You must prevent your heart from signing out before you have reasoned through the concrete facts. Do not let a limited paradigm keep you from tapping into the greatest resource for your organization. Do you really want to belittle the best thing you have going for you? I challenge you: **don't** err from a heart full of pride. Study the benefits of this principle. You will only add to your knowledge and abilities.

SECTION I: The Power of Simplicity

As mentioned in the e-book of *The Capwise Leader, & The Ten Powers of Principles,* I have no intention of telling you the first principle. The first principle or truth is the foundation from where all other principles originate. I can tell you that it is far greater than the second principle. I hope with all my heart that you search for the first principle. If you search for it, you will find it. As the second principle is applied with greater and greater accuracy you will experience manifold bounty in your business. Your desire to find the first principle should also increase.

Not a Strategy and Not a Philosophy

The title of the book says it all. We are going to look at a principle that is neither a strategy nor a philosophy. This principle contains all 10 powers described in the e-book, *The Capwise Leader, & The Ten Powers of Principles.* The second principle is so powerful it will take a whole book just to scratch the surface!

Not a Strategy

The second principle is the power behind all successful business strategies ever used in world history. It is the fundamental foundation to all success in every field of leadership. This principle is not a strategy, but leads to all successful strategies. That is the greatness of the Second Principle. CAP is another way to say strategy. I want to empower you with the ability to develop your **own** strategies by understanding what makes a leadership plan successful. **You** are completely capable of leading your organization to new levels of achievement.

What this means to you is...
There are an infinite number of successful and powerful strategies you can design for yourself and see greater results in your business!

Not a Philosophy

The most pragmatic, sequential thinking person in the world will see the rationale behind the second principle. This principle is entirely concrete and has so many ways to measure its CAP.

What this means to you is...
You can measure your progress in time, people and money! You can see the difference in ownership and responsibility of your followers. You can numerically measure the productivity of your employees. The bottom line will measure your increased profits. It all starts with the second principle.

Two Types of Principles

There are two types of principles in creation: physical principles and moral principles.

When used correctly, physical principles, such as the law of aerodynamics, create many new opportunities and benefits for mankind. We can fly from state to state in a few hours, because we learned to obey the aerodynamic laws that pre-existed the first plane.

The more one obeys the moral principles/laws, which existed long before any two people decided to work together for a common cause, the more potential success the business can experience!

Paper Airplanes and Leaders

Principles cannot be "seen" until they are used. Physical principles cannot be measured until one tries to use them. Let's do a profound experiment. Take a sheet of paper from your printer and without changing its size or shape toss it as far as you can.

How far did it go?
Did it glide easily to the other end of the room?

The reason it did not soar into the wild blue yonder is because of physical principles. The paper was not designed to use the aerodynamic principles to its favor. The shape and weight of the paper were designed in such a way to fight against natural principles that could otherwise have carried it across the room.

Take the same piece of paper and crunch it up into a tight little ball. Now toss it as far as you can.

How far did the ball go?
How much effort did it take to get some real distance?

The ball shape does a better job obeying the aerodynamic laws, but in order to get substantial distance, you must work harder. A lot of personal effort is used to get the desired distance.

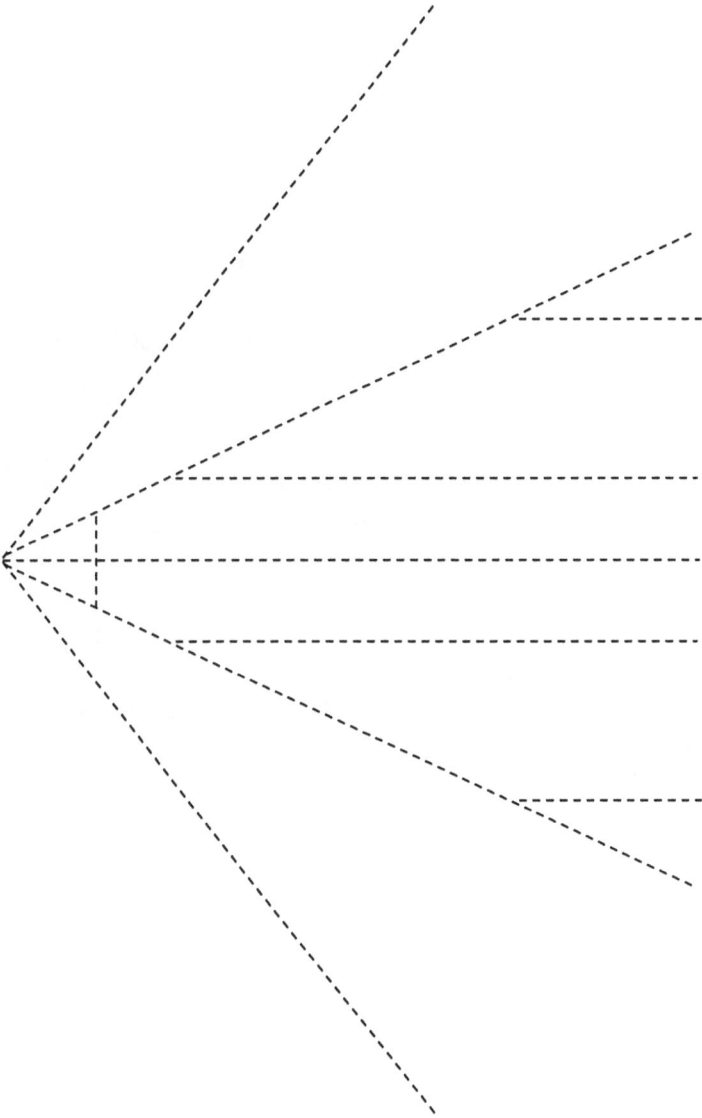

Use the pattern provided to build a paper airplane. Now toss the plane into the air.
How far did it go?

How much energy did you use to propel the plane?
How much control did you have in the direction of the plane?
Do you think with practice you could achieve longer, smoother sustained flights with your paper airplane?

The power to use the principles that caused the plane to glide was easily harnessed by simply folding a piece of paper *the correct way.* A paper airplane is a correct application of a principle (CAP).

Plane Directions

Moral principles can also be applied correctly or incorrectly. If applied incorrectly, your business will look like the piece of paper tossed into the air. There will be no control, no extended flight, and a messy landing. Use your head and use your heart. The ability to ride on the winds of moral principles is currently within your reach. I am sure you are already using many moral principles correctly. By the end of this book you will learn about the most important principle to apply to your business or organization. Think about how you can use this principle to its greatest advantage, and make a profound difference in the success of your organization!

The Golden Rule

"Do unto others as you would have them do unto you."

The Golden Rule is a sentence description of **love**. *The Golden Rule* is so absolute that it is the principle that has allowed all civilizations to survive and thrive. Consider the ancient Roman world. The Romans are famous for a government of the people and for the people. Many attribute the fall of Rome to the complete degradation of their moral fortitude. Politicians and rulers became self-seeking to the point of their own destruction.

For all you pragmatics out there who believe the second principle is a warm, fuzzy and useless idea that has no relevance in the world today, please keep reading. We will focus on the hard facts of this principle, and then we will take a closer look at your heart.

This principle is truly **Golden** in every way. Correctly applied, *The Golden Rule* will unleash the productivity and profitability in your organization!

The application of *The Golden Rule* is completely measurable in time, people and money.

All business problems in the world originate from an incorrect application of *The Golden Rule*.

Why is Enron so famous? Would you say that the leaders were thinking of their employees?

Consider Scott Paper Company as Albert Dunlap found it when he became the leader. Exorbitant amounts of money (hard-earned money from the employees) were going directly for a posh lifestyle of its leaders. The leaders were enjoying a corporate jet, luxury headquarters, and annual salaries indifferent to their performance. There was a complete disconnection between the leaders and the followers. How well do you think Scott was applying *The Golden Rule* before Al arrived?

Consider Jack Welch, CEO of GE. One of his main goals was to FREE middle management from bureaucracy. This action created ownership and responsibility thus improving the productivity and profitability of the company. CAP creates true freedom; freedom **of** responsibility. Jack had been in middle management and knew what it felt like. So when he arrived at the top he began to improve his CAP of *The Golden Rule*; it was the KEY to the future success of GE!

Albert Dunlap and Jack Welch are classic examples of leaders unleashing the power of *The Golden Rule.* The CAP of *The Golden Rule* is highly measurable. A leader can measure the results in time, money, and people. An obvious example is customer service. As the leader, your team of followers had better know exactly what great customer service looks like, because it is guaranteed your customers will know.

The P.O.O.P. Cycle

Let's start with the negative effects of **P**oorly **O**rganized and **O**rchestrated use of **P**rinciples: P.O.O.P. When customer service is poor, what are the results for your business? You have the loss of first-time customers and then you have the loss of repeat customers, which results in lost sales. Let's say a leader happens to be "reactive" and has a bad case of the "knee-jerks." He reacts by having a meeting with all his employees and gives them a quasi-reprimand and quasi-customer service training. There is a spirit of disappointment emanating from the leader towards the followers. He is also angered with the followers because they didn't intuitively know what excellent customer service looks like. The followers feel disappointed. One follower is so hurt he decides he does not have to put up being belittled— so he quits. Let's take a moment and count the financial costs of this simple example. In your business you would know the cost of each item. Feel free to list the monetary value for three lost customers.

Loss of three new customers   = $_____?

Loss of three repeat customers   = $_____?

Cost of "leader-reactive" employee training

Loss of work time due to training. = $_____?

Cost for training and materials.
Business Consultant   = $_____?
Cost for refreshments   = $_____?

Total for "leader-reactive" employee training

= $_____?

Loss of Employee Costs

Loss of time while training new employee
= $_____?

Cost of over-time for other employees to fill gap
= $_____?

Cost of advertising for new employee
= $_____?

Cost in time of leader to interview new employee
= $_____?

Cost for training new employee
= $_____?

Let's add a few more costs due to **P.O.O.P.** The reprimand from the leader during the training makes the followers skittish because they were never given a clearly defined expectation of customer service. Now they are getting yelled at for doing something wrong.

From the perspective of the followers they were blindsided by their leader who claims to have "known all along" what good customer service looks like. There is a sense of betrayal and the followers lose trust in the leader. Lack of trust leads to lack of safety in the job for fear of being punished. Followers now spend more time and energy protecting themselves and playing it safe. Consequently, less effort is given to the organization.

How much do you think it will cost your business to have your employees afraid to go the extra mile? Do the math. What total costs are you coming up with? The whole scenario seems so complicated. Certainly there must be an equally complicated solution.

The problem is complicated.
The solution is **simple**!

Correctly apply *The Golden Rule* in every area of your business. The CAP begins with the leader. Everything else is cause and effect.

The #1 challenge for every business leader is finding and hiring the "right" employees. *The Second Most Powerful Principle in the Universe* is **inter-relational**.
The #1 challenge for every business leader is a relational challenge, not a business problem.

The CAP of *The Golden Rule* in your business affects every corner of your operation. CAP increases vision and unity, resulting in increased morale and effort. The end result is increased productivity and profitability. It's that simple, but it has to start with the leader!

The Big Picture

The Golden Rule is **SO POWERFUL** that every business and non-profit organization in the world uses it as their fundamental principle. This is clearly seen when one realizes that every business and organization in the world is an expression of some kind of service to mankind. I can guarantee your business has a purpose to serve mankind with a product or service. Your business is making money by helping other people!

You might be the owner of a wire fabrication factory. That wire will be part of batteries for cars, which people will rely on in the middle of winter. You might be the supervisor of a water treatment plant. In today's "green" thinking one might say you are helping nature; but in reality, you are serving mankind by keeping the water clean. I hope you see the clear pattern built into creation. If you can make money serving other people, then you can make more money by applying *The Golden Rule* more precisely within your business.

PRINCIPLES

1. Universal	6. Lowest Common Denominator
2. Timeless	7. Inter-Relational
3. Not Age Biased	8. Creates Freedom & Safety
4. Infinite	9. FREE!
5. Binary	10. Foundation of Wisdom

The 10 Powers of *The Golden Rule*

1. Universal

The Golden Rule is used on every corner of the world. It is used by every human organization on the earth; some use it better than others. It is used from little league baseball to world-wide corporations, from Tupperware parties to the United Nations (UN). Ok, the UN is stretching it, but really, the entire purpose of the UN is based upon *The Golden Rule*. One might challenge the CAP of the UN, but that does not change its primary principle.

What this means to you is...
You are already using the principle with some degree of success. You have no choice but to use it. Your goal to be the best leader you can be is to embrace this principle with your whole heart and soul, and let it take your business to new heights.

---

2. Timeless

The Second Principle will always be the foundation of your business. No matter how big your organization grows, *The Golden Rule* will grow with you. The CAP or strategies will develop as needed. The Second Principle never changes, but your application of it will increase and improve the longer you use it.

> **What this means to you is...**
> You can trust that no matter how much things change within your organization, the Second Principle will never change and you will have a constant companion growing in power. The power will always be greater than your need.

3. Not Age Biased

The Golden Rule is not age biased. You might be a brand new, fresh-out-of-school leader. You can use this principle just as freely as a 60-year-old CEO of a large corporation. The challenge the young leader will face is a false idea that one must build a business first and then apply the Second Principle later. That is inversed thinking. Apply *The Golden Rule* with the best of your ability and you will build a better business right from the start.

> **What this means to you is...**
> Always start with the basics first! The greater power is in establishing the fundamentals correctly.

4. Infinite Power

I know this is starting to sound more like a sci-fi movie, but the truth is *The Golden Rule* is infinite. There will never be a time when your business or organization will no longer need or use the Second Principle. Your organization will always need the power of *The Golden Rule*. As your organization grows so will the principle. A constant source of energy will always be available to move your business forward.

What this means to you is...
The better you learn to use *The Golden Rule*, the better off your business will be. The Second Principle will always have more than enough to carry your organization to greater levels of achievement.

---

5. Binary

The Golden Rule is the beginning, foundational, and fundamental principle that exists. All other principles are established from the Second Principle, and make no mistake—this is THE ONE AND ONLY Second Principle. There are no other principles of equal or greater power and worth except for the First Principle.

All businesses and organizations, and all leaders and followers are subservient to *The Golden Rule*, whether they use it correctly or incorrectly. The better a leader understands and establishes *The Golden Rule*, the better a leader will apply all other leadership and organizational principles.

> **What this means to you is...**
> As a leader improves their CAP of
> *The Golden Rule*, there will be no
> limit to the effectiveness and outcome
> in their business or organization!

6. Lowest Common Denominator

It's all about the basics. Don't let all your education, methods and theories dilute the obvious! Don't get lost in a mountain of leadership help books that offer convoluted strategies and practices of "leadership".

If you cannot clearly identify and apply *The Golden Rule* to perfection all other efforts are irrelevant. Keep it simple; keep it clean; and stick to the basics. Always start with the simplest solution. I can guarantee that most of the business problems in the world are due to people not following *The Golden Rule*.

Leadership does not get more fundamental than *The Golden Rule*. The Second Principle is the foundational bedrock for all successful leaders! Let *The Golden Rule* permeate your heart and mind and you will notice a huge difference in your ability to influence people!

> **What this means to you is...**
> The greatest improvement you can
> make as a leader is already within
> your grasp. It is doing the simple stuff
> right.

7. Inter-Relational

As a leader, you already have all the resource you will ever need to correctly apply the Second Principle in your organization. The two primary elements of *The Golden Rule* are (i) you; and (ii) anybody else. Two or more people and time are the basic ingredients to correctly apply this principle.

The Second Principle is inter-relational, which means that without you it will not work. To tap into the greatest power available to your business requires that this power comes directly from you, the leader. Are you willing to see your business grow in morale, unity, ownership, productivity, and profitability? It will take a personal commitment from you to improve your CAP of the Second Principle. The CAP of *The Golden Rule* will be discussed in the section entitled Open Heart Surgery, **O.H.S**.

What this means to you is...
The best tools to achieve greater success in your organization you already possess:
you and your people.

---

8. Safety & 9. Freedom

A powerful product of *The Golden Rule* is that it creates safety and freedom, for you and the people of your organization. If you want more ownership from your employees, the Second Principle is the only way to go. Ownership comes from feeling safe to give more heart and the freedom to pursue the ownership. Ownership is freedom **of** responsibility not **from** responsibility. It all begins with the leader. If your CAP of *The Golden Rule* is truly correct, you will be instilling safety and freedom for your followers to work harder for the business. The safety and freedom in your organization is a direct result of your leadership. Your ability to CAP the Second Principle will directly affect the productivity and profitability of your organization.

What this means to you is...
When you and your followers feel
safe and free at work,
everyone will work harder!

---

10. The second Most Powerful Principle in the Universe is FREE!

I think it is important to look at the big picture for just a moment. This is truth. There is something in the world that will greatly enhance every aspect of your organization. It has limitless power, is very simple to use, empowers your organization to achieve more, improves the work environment in every possible way, is already being used to some degree in your organization, and it happens to be FREE. You can't beat that deal!

What this means to you is...
The R.O.I. of *The Golden Rule*
is **priceless!**

The Golden Rule can be stopped!

There is only one barrier that has the power to slow down, hinder, and even cause the Second Principle to work in reverse. That barrier is the human heart. I am not referring to the physical organ that pumps blood. I am referring to the emotional and spiritual part of a human; one's character.

Now it's Getting Personal

The heart of the leader is the most powerful tool in every business because the heart of the leader controls the CAP of *The Golden Rule*. It is not the followers'/employees' job to control the CAP of the Second Principle. The proper use of *The Golden Rule* is the entire responsibility of the leader. This is where the rubber meets the road. What is coming next is your opportunity to find out how you might be hindering the progress of your own business.

You, "the leader," might be the biggest barrier to greater levels of productivity and profit. Your inherent character traits might be the one thing that is tripping up the very plans you set into motion. You might be a self-saboteur. That does not mean you should start looking for your replacement, but it does mean it is time to be an over-comer of yourself!

Common Examples of Leadership Self-Sabotage

Manipulation instead of Influence
Politicking instead of Empowering
Enforce instead of Encourage

The fundamental difference in the list above is the application of *The Golden Rule*. Manipulation, politics, and enforcing are all selfish actions leading to poor leadership and poor results.

Poorly **O**rganized and **O**rchestrated use of a **P**rinciple: P.O.O.P. The focus of P.O.O.P. is SELF at the cost of all others.

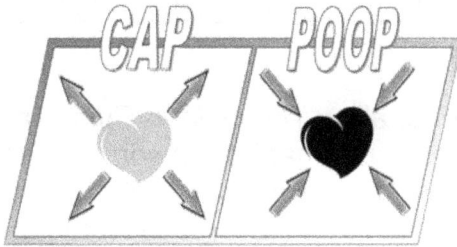

The **C**orrect **A**pplication of **P**rinciples: CAP of *The Golden Rule* in fundamental leadership is Influence, Empowerment, and Encouragement. The focus of CAP is OTHERS at the cost of self.

Now we come to the heart of the matter (pun intended). It is the heart of the leader that determines the expression of *The Golden Rule*, and consequently, the performance of your business. The heart of the leader will determine if *The Golden Rule* will be CAPed or POOPed.

SECTION II: O.H.S. (Open Heart Surgery)

In order to allow *The Golden Rule* to be expressed more freely into your organization you must take a closer look at your own heart. Be honest with yourself. This is not a touchy-feely time. This is taking a closer look at the fact that you might be the one slowing down the growth of your own business. There is no one to blame but yourself for the internal problems your organization may have.

The #1 challenge in most businesses is believed to be the employees. You might be an entrepreneur, or a CEO, but the toughest challenge you will face is working with other people. I have heard leaders state that people don't have the same work ethic anymore, but that is simply a sad excuse for poor leadership. The fact is nothing has ever changed. People are still people. There is no such thing as the "good ol' days." People react defensively to poor leadership, and react positively to good leadership. People can and will do the impossible with superior leadership. What type of leader do you want to be?

A Vicious Cycle

The followers in any organization can sniff out a selfish leader immediately. The moment the heart of the leader is exposed to be selfish; the trust factor drops through the floor. The followers prepare their own hearts for poor leadership. That means your employees take valuable time and energy that could be used to benefit the business and use that valuable energy to protect themselves. The followers must use precious energy to protect themselves from the leader, and the business suffers. How is that for an irony? But wait it gets worse!

The typical pattern of the selfish leader is more P.O.O.P. The selfish leader sees that employees are not giving all that they can and the business is not producing.

P.O.O.P. is called upon to make the difference. The leader REACTS with a serious case of "knee-jerks" and calls upon the authority of his position to make the change.

First the leader uses the tried and true method: "throw the dog a bone," to win over the followers. The leader gives everyone a gift certificate to a restaurant. The followers gobble up the gift, but have no idea why it was given and the distrust continues.

Next, the leader brings in middle management and gives them false freedom, with no clear direction, to manage the followers so they might produce more. Little does middle management know that the "Hangman's Leash" has just been placed around their neck. Middle management, excited with their new found responsibility and trust, dives into their jobs with more passion. Suddenly they are called into the office and reprimanded for doing something "wrong." Dazed and confused they wander back to the role of status quo, not daring to take the risk of initiative again.

The leader now calls upon the powers of politics and manipulation to win people over to his side. Middle management and the followers who want get ahead begin to emulate more politicking and manipulation. Distrust and selfish gain is now the name of the game. The organization becomes a "dog-eat-dog" culture and the production and profits suffer.

In a dog-eat-dog world, the leader **must** be the "Alpha Dog!" Someone has to be the "heavy" for anything to get done.
"Do it because I said so." No questions—just obedience. You are not paid to think; just obey. Forget giving responsibility to the follower—obey your leader or there's the door! The leader is the alpha dog and middle management jockey for position in the pecking order. Production decreases, and profits suffer.

"Time to Lean, Time to Clean!"

Next, the leader has a meeting with all middle management and blames them for poor leadership. The "got time to lean, got time to clean" policy goes into effect. Anyone "caught" not being busy will be driven back to work. Middle management, finally given clear direction with parameters, does what they are told to the letter. Employee morale goes down as people feel belittled and used. Distrust goes up, production goes down, and the employees that can afford it, leave for greener pastures.

The example of the vicious cycle looks very complicated. It would seem that a complex plan would be needed to break this unproductive behavior pattern. One might think that it is time to call in the professional consultants to unravel the mess. The real solution to this type of organizational mess is quite simple, but it must start with the leader. The leader must grasp the powers of *The Golden Rule* and put it to work, but it MUST begin with the top leader—anything less is only patch work.

The most important business tool the leader has to work with is their heart. It is the heart of the leader that will determine the CAP of *The Golden Rule*. However, it is important to first acknowledge other fundamental business challenges that are common to the leader.

Pseudo Dichotomies! (False Division)

Pseudo Dichotomy #1
Leaders lead businesses not a community club.

What type of business do you lead?

What business do you own?

What product or service do you produce, and for whom?

I bet you answered those questions with clarity and detail, but do you realize the simplicity of your true role? The correct answer for every leader in every business and organization is this.

You are a **person** who leads **people** to serve **people. Fundamentally; the team approach to *The Golden Rule***

Your Real Career

Principles are always the lowest common denominator. You may think you are the vice president or the CEO of a corporation that makes diodes for electronics all around the world. You may think you are the owner and operator of a pizza shop with five employees. That is where most leaders get confused. Most leaders think they are business leaders, but **ALL** leaders are **people leaders,** not business leaders. When the leader, excited about their business, finds themselves in a struggle leading people, they become confused.

Managers think:
"This job would be great if it weren't for the people."

Ministers think:
"Being a minister would be so much easier if it weren't for the people."

Entrepreneurs think:
"My start-ups would be so much more successful if it weren't for the people."

Entrepreneurs are often taken by surprise when their independent, self-reliant passions result in being the center of a group of people.

When the leader is confused, they struggle with the tension of managing people **OR** running the business. In their minds there is a dichotomy between one and the other. Managing people and running the business are two sides of the same coin. The leader must balance both roles. As the organization grows, the leader usually delegates various responsibilities to managers and supervisors. It is important to note that the leader will never be able to separate the people work from the planning work. The leader will always have the management team to lead, person to person.

The pseudo dichotomy is a confusion of what one's business does as a service and the REAL goal to serve people.

Pseudo Dichotomy #2
The real goal of my business is to make money.

The real goal of every business in the whole world is to serve people.

One might think the goal is to make money, but the profits of a business are the byproducts of good CUSTOMER SERVICE *or* PEOPLE SERVICE. You may have a business to business or a business to consumer organization. In a business to business service, who makes up the other business? People! If you do not do a good job serving others with your business, whether it is making a quality product or offering a quality service, your business will not make money.

In order to make the most amount of money in your business you must offer the best quality service. In order to have top quality service you must have top quality people helping you achieve your goal. In order to have top quality people working for your business you must lead people with superior quality.

Jeff Blackman, a Business Growth Specialist, shares insight from Fred Smith a leader of Fed Ex.

Jeff states, "The leaders acknowledge employee satisfaction as the primary corporate objective."

In his *Opportunity Selling* audio series Jeff quotes Fred Smith, who states, "When people are placed first, they will provide the highest possible service and profits will follow." The people referred to in the quote are the **employees** of Fed Ex.

So when you experience problems from your employees or volunteers, just remember that you are a person, who is in a position to lead people, and to serve people. **You are a people leader, not a business leader**. Keep it simple, keep it focused, and watch your business succeed. Lead your people to new levels of superior customer service, which in return, produces differentiation as a business, which in return produces higher profits!

What this means to you is…
If you do not plan every action of your day with the understanding that you are a people leader and not a business leader, you are hurting your own business.

Pseudo Dichotomy #3
There is a time for work, and a time for fun

Work is a necessary evil so you can pursue the things you really enjoy.

If the leader has this dichotomy built into their philosophy of work, they will produce followers with the same philosophy. If work is a necessary evil then it is impossible for a follower to work with all their heart. If a person doesn't believe in their work, they will not produce as much as they could. Do you really want your followers to dread the thought of working for you and your business? How do you think "the dreaded job" mentality will affect productivity from your followers?

Pseudo Dichotomy #4
Ego and Fear vs. Confidence and Courage

I still hear many experts say that leaders need to have a big ego in order to be a good leader. I will suggest leaders need to have Confidence and Courage in who they are and their abilities. Ego is selfish pride in one's talents and gifts and is fundamentally self-centered. Ego is always followed by fear that one may lose their prestigious position and power, because ego is fundamentally **selfish**.

Confidence is a humble acceptance of the gifts and talents one has been given and the sense of responsibility to use it for the good of others. It takes Courage to recognize and pursue responsibility. Confidence is fundamentally **selfless**. Think of Spiderman's prime directive:

"With Great Power
Comes Great Responsibility."

What this means to you is...
If you have an ego, you'd better do what you can to kill it as fast as possible if you want your business to succeed further. It will take courage to let go of something you believe you need to protect. If you spend all your time protecting your power and position, then you are not using that power and position to grow your organization.

Let's Get Personal

It's all about the leader's heart.

> Do you really know how you treat people?
> How do you really see people?
> How do you feel about people?
> Do you trust people?
> Do you trust your managers, your employees?

The truth is every business leader in the world is really a people leader. It is also true that how the leader perceives people is how they will treat them.

How you see'em is how you will treat'em.

How do you perceive people? Are people mindless cattle to be lead to market? Do you see them as ravenous wolves waiting to take your position from you?

Are people the greatest asset you have going for your business? How do you really feel about people?

Are you the type of leader that leaves a body count behind you when people leave your office? Do women leave your office crying? Do men make a noted effort to avoid you?

Is there such a thing as brainstorming in a meeting or is everything a debate to be won or lost?

Do you perceive that any one who disagrees with you is wrong and must be defeated?

If you said yes to these questions then there is a good chance you are a leader bound with fear.

In the book, *The Capwise Leader & The Ten Powers of Principles*, power #8 states that principles create freedom.

Is your heart free to lead people? Go to Capwiseleader.com and get your copy.

Real freedom carries real responsibility. You are the leader of the people within your business. You have the title and all the responsibilities to see that business succeed. If your heart is not free to lead your people, then your business will suffer in every way.

People
Perceived as your greatest asset

What does a leader need to be free from?

FEAR

Fear causes a leader to act defensively in every situation that he or she interprets as a threat to self.

When one of your followers comes to you to suggest an improvement, do you reinterpret that as blaming you for doing something wrong?

A heart bound by fear is a heart of self-protection. A self-protecting heart CANNOT be selfless, because it feels

35

its very survival is at stake. Defend and attack. Preemptive strikes and counter-attacks stay at the top no matter what and no matter who becomes a casualty of war. Nothing personal—it's just business. A heart bound by fear cannot apply *The Golden Rule*, because it is directly opposed to the principle.

People
Perceived as your greatest liability

Here's a true story. There was a head nurse leading a team of nurses for a hospital. The head nurse was bound by fear and was always lashing out at her team because she was afraid they always wanted to challenge her authority.

She was constantly exhibiting actions of distrust towards her team. Consequently, her team responded with distrust. So she held an in-service and hired an outside business consulting firm to speak. The topic was, "How to Treat Your Leader." What effect do you think that in-service had on the followers?

A selfish heart cannot be a selfless heart. In order to use the powers of *The Golden Rule* you must free your heart of selfishness. You must become a real leader. Removing selfishness is a process that does not happen all at once. The clue is in the name: it is a process.

Pseudo Dichotomy #5
Plateau vs. Process

This is the all or nothing attitude, or the adult version of a childish fit.
"If it can't be done like this, then let's not do it at all!"

A leader must have the patience to train, guide, and coach their followers. No one is going to be an expert right from the start. It is a process to train people to a preferred level of productivity. Guide people, show them the big picture. Show your followers how they contribute to the success of the organization.

The same is true for your own growth as a leader. Growth is a process that has no plateau. Growth is a never-ending journey.

If you do an honest inventory of your heart and find a lot of selfishness, there is probably a good reason you have it. Look back over your past. Have there been times in your past leadership experiences when you were blindsided by someone whose sole purpose was to accuse you of something? Most likely in your past you were severely hurt by another leader or one of your followers. Your very character was attacked and it seemed that the only purpose was to destroy you and take away your dignity.

The Vow
Usually after a painful experience a person makes the Vow. The Vow is a commitment to protect oneself from future pain.

"I will never let them hurt me again!"

In most cases the Vow is a series of defensive measures the leader builds around their heart. The leader makes a promise never to be caught off-guard again. Any time the heart believes an experience is potentially threatening, the leader reacts to counteract the event, even before it happens. The whole motivation of the heart is SELF-defense and SELF-focus. One cannot be a good leader who is SELF-focused for any reason.

The Vow usually causes the same events to happen again and again. Here comes another cycle of P.O.O.P. A self-focused leader will do actions trying to protect their heart. Those actions come across to the followers as distrust and inability to lead. Thus followers react with fear and distrust and either avoid the leader at all cost, or look for reason to accuse the leader.

Take a moment to think about how this will effect the operations of the company. Many leaders, who are bound by fear, are also afraid of losing their job. Does the P.O.O.P. cycle described above increase the chances of losing your job or improve your job security?

You have to come to your senses and realize that defensive, self-focused leadership does not work. You must decide to move out from your walls of self-protection and take chances again and again.

In order to break the P.O.O.P. cycle of poor leadership you must free your heart of fear, and find the courage to move towards your followers for **THEIR** benefit. Somehow you must find the courage to CAP *The Golden Rule*.

Let's follow the path of *The Golden Rule*. As we look at this path of goals, listen as your heart begins to come up with its own leadership strategies.

Service or Product from a Business/Organization/Church

1. Goal: Excellent customer service. Every customer must feel they have been treated with superior care. "*The Golden Rule.*"

What would excellent customer service look like in your business? What are three things you could do to improve customer service?

2. Goal: Equip followers to provide superior customer service.

What do your followers need in order to provide superior care?

What can you do to make sure your followers give more than a service, and give from their heart?

What are five things you can do to provide your followers the freedom and ability to give from their heart?

3. Goal: Consider what you must do to give yourself the freedom to give your followers what they need.

This is the most important question because it is the first cause. The principle of cause and effect begins with the leader. You must be the first expression of superior customer service.

A very good motivator when striving for greater leadership is to think about the personal benefits you will gain when your business or organization achieves new levels of productivity and profitability. Set measurable quantitative goals. It is not selfish motivation to enjoy the fruits of success.

Is it selfish motivation to enjoy the honeymoon after a long engagement? No, the honeymoon is the consummation of a worthy pursuit. The same holds true in the business world. I am sure you have a worthy product or service that is going to make the world a better place. People want your product or service and they are willing to pay money for it. Your organization is creating a win/win situation.

This is where things get confusing. Navigating ones own heart is the scariest and most confusing journey a person can make. You may be the toughest leader in town, but I can guarantee you that there are parts of your heart that have you running scared.

Consider the "choleric," a typical and common character trait. Have you ever noticed how the strong choleric types are easily angered? Anger is usually their prominent emotional response to just about anything. Choleric types have the very same reaction to being hurt as every other leader. They build defenses to protect themselves from being hurt. Make no mistake—their heart is just as sensitive as everybody else's. They just throw out anger as a way to protect themselves, just like an octopus blows out a cloud of ink so it can escape. Anger is a smoke-screen so the choleric can run in fear.

Poor Leadership Strategies of a Defensive Heart
(Signs that change is in order.)

If you see these following strategies in your leadership you are most likely struggling with a defensive, self-focused heart, and are damaging the success of your organization.

The Alpha Dog, Enforcer
"Do as I say, because I am the leader."

"I'm the Boss, do as I say!"

If you feel you have to "posture" yourself as the head honcho, then you probably struggle with a strong inferiority complex. The moment you have to tell your followers that you are the leader you lose your leadership. If you feel you have to throw your title at people in order for them to work for you, there is a serious lack of true influencing power.

"Someone has got to be the heavy, the bad guy." This is a heart that does not know how to connect with their followers and lead them to strive for greater results.

The Knee-Jerk; Reactor
"Quick! Change it NOW; I don't care how!"

A common sign of defensive leadership is the knee-jerk reaction to criticism and problems. A knee-jerk reaction is a blind unthinking response to run from the problem. Instead of looking at the problem, and tracing it back to the real roots, the leader tries to remove the problem by a shortcut and never really looks at the deeper issues. No time is given to a thorough investigation of what is leading to the problem, just fix it!

Quick React, Don't think about it!

Examples of Reactors

1.   **Poor customer service**. Quick, hire a third-party organization to hold an in-service. Topic: customer service.

2.   **Criticism**. Quick, comply for the complainer, whether they are right or wrong. (Ministers are very susceptible to this one).

3.   **Chew'em Out**. Quick, get into my office. "What the heck were you thinking?!" When you bring in your

follower for a 'reprimand' what you really are telling them is, "I knew better than that, why didn't you?" You are guaranteed to lose the heart of your follower. That type of reaction exposes one's inability to lead, not just the follower's inability to follow.

Hangman's Leash

"I'll give you just enough leash to hang yourself, Then I will call you into the office for a reprimand."

This is a really bad leadership strategy. Any follower with an ounce of dignity is going to respond very poorly to the leash. The hangman's leash is the opposite of leadership. Leadership gives guidance and protection. The hangman's leash gives ambiguity and no protection at all. The follower makes a mistake and feels bad about it. Then the leader kicks the follower when they are down.

Punch in the Gut; *BUT*
"You are doing great job, BUT here's the problem."

"You have nice handwriting BUT!"

Many times the leader wants to soften the blow and be kind to the follower so before they reprimand the follower they say something nice first. The effect on the follower is like a punch in the gut. Have the follower stand up straight and tall with something nice and then WHAM, slug'em in the gut, and as they double over in pain and gasp for air, the leader tells them their failures.

Throw the Dog a Bone
"I will win the trust of my followers with a random gift for obedience."

"Did you like my random gift?"

Have you ever tried to make friends with a scared dog? If you were to offer a scared dog a t-bone steak, it will take the steak and enjoy it, but it will still keep one eye on you. That is exactly how followers will respond when they don't trust their leader. If the followers do not trust the leaders, they might take the gift but that won't increase their trust. The smarter followers may not even take the gift for fear it may be a trap. The trap they are afraid of is called *implied obligation*. "If I take this gift, I will be obligated to do more."

Politicking
Divide and conquer, win key people over to "your side."

If a leader feels the need to politic, then there are already divisions within the organization. The leader is driving the divisions by playing sides. That also means the leader has followers who are **not** following.

The leader needs to bridge divisions—not encourage them. When divisions are played against each other, there will be winners and losers. There is nothing wrong with healthy competition between two opposing teams or businesses, but when there is division on the **same** team there will be winners and losers, but the **whole** team loses the game. Politicking uses the tools of manipulation and debate. Manipulation breeds distrust, and debate breeds division.

Slave Driver
"Got time to lean; got time clean."

"Got time to gripe, got time to type!"

    This poor strategy is prominent in middle management. The middle manager is afraid of how they will be perceived by their leader, so they make sure the followers are always busy—maybe not always productive, but always busy. The assumption is busyness means productivity. The idea is the top leader walks by on the way to the coffee machine, sees all the busy followers, and thinks middle management is doing their job.

    The followers feel like cattle being poked and prodded every time they rest for a moment. It is a belittling method for humans and produces distrust, anger, and resentment towards the leader. Have you ever noticed in the movies that slave-driving is what the bad guys always do?

    In all the examples listed, the prime cause is always constant. The leader is focused on self. None of the poor strategies has the best interest of the followers in mind. The leader may fool themselves into thinking that they know what is best for the business and with no business the followers have no job. "If you want to have a job, just do as I say."

The real issue with many businesses is that the leader is the cause for many of the organizational problems. The leader creates problems and then feeds them. The leader becomes a self-fulfilling prophecy by reacting to the problems he/she has created. This is a vicious cycle that only the leader can break because it begins with the leader. The cycle is simple to see. A self-protective leader will produce self-protecting followers, which will produce very little.

The Gold of *The Golden Rule*

The paradoxical truth is if you want to protect yourself, you must sacrifice yourself for the good of others. In return others will give more to your organization in response to your amazing leadership. Followers will produce more and increase the success of the business for **all to benefit**. A selfless leader will produce selfless followers which will produce beyond all expectation!

A "pseudo" reason not to placate

A common fear of self-protective leaders is the fear of placating the follower. Obviously it is never good to placate people. The self-protective leader has a fear of placating that is really the fear of inferiority. Inferiority is the fear of allowing the follower to ever be right or take the one up position over the leader on any issue.

The leader may think, "The follower must not be allowed to think that they are right and I am wrong."
Placating is falsely perceived as an act of submission and a selfish leader would rather die than submit and possibly be wrong.

A real reason not to placate

Placating is a form of manipulation that deceives the follower and steals their dignity. Placating is built on the premise of a one up one down model. The leader who is one up, strokes the follower, who is one down. The leader believes they are so clever for stroking the ego or "allowing" the follower to believe the follower owns the idea, when all the time it was part of the leader's clever plan to take over the world. *Whoa, Ha Ha Ha!*

Again, it all comes right back to the heart of the leader. How the leader perceives their people is how they will treat them. A leader that thinks placating is a tool to use, simply thinks they "know" better than their follower.

A leader will think, "I will guide you, my simple and lowly servant, for I know what is best, and I am doing this for your own good."

"My humble servant, you are so simple you don't even realize I have just manipulated you to do what I want, but it is for the better."

Would you want to follow a leader who thinks of you in that way?

You must continuously free your heart to use the power of *The Golden Rule* in ever increasing and effective ways.

SECTION III: CAP *The Golden Rule*

How to CAP The Golden Rule

This book has what you need before you read all the other leadership books. Other leadership books talk about strategies or applications of principles without clearly defining the principles.

What this means to you is...
A clear understanding of principles increases your focus on the right goals. The more clearly you understand your true role as a leader, the easier it is to focus your efforts. It is very refreshing to know exactly what you are pursuing for the day. You know when you have achieved your goal.
It is very liberating to have a clear pursuit of progress.

Most leadership books mention the fruit of the strategies as the justification for applying the strategies. There are some books that claim leadership principles, but describe applications of principles. It is important to note that these are all great books and I highly recommend reading many leadership books. It is also important to note that there are fundamental, universal principles that are the launching pad for all business strategies. When a leader clearly understands fundamental truth, strategies become self-evident. It does not take an outside expert to show the way, if the leader is willing to do the hard work of understanding principles.

Correct Application of Principles (CAP) looks like...
Golf!

Consider golfing for a moment. There are different clubs to achieve different goals with the ball. There are irons, and there are woods. You gather the best clubs you can afford and then you practice. You study ever minutiae of your body: the way you stand, the way you hold your clubs, the way you swing. You keep adjusting these postures and actions and you notice the results of each swing. A little straighter and a little further is the goal until you learn to put the ball where you want it. It is the same with principles. You gather as many principles as you can. You then learn how to use the principles and improve the results in your business.

The more effective you can apply a principle, the greater the results for your organization. Other leadership books will give you some great applications of principles and thus speed up the process. Just like having your own personal coach for golf can save time, money and frustration. That is the wonderful effect of OPE, Other, Peoples, Experiences, their pain is your gain, and your gain of experiential leverage will move you that much further ahead.

The Heart of the Matter

It is important to understand that how you perceive your followers is how you will treat them. If you believe the people in your organization are the biggest pain in the butt, then that is how you will treat them.

Your first goal, change your heart! (Now would be a good time to go looking for the first most powerful principle in the universe.)

You can begin applying *The Golden Rule* correctly even with a hurt and defensive heart. The paradoxical truth is, to correctly apply *The Golden Rule* **you** must get out of the way. To do to others as you would have them do to you, you must gather certain tools to help you get out of the way.

What type of tools do you need to successfully apply *The Golden Rule*? The one primary tool you will need is a **healing heart**.

Every human in the world has been hurt by others in some way or another. You don't need a "healed heart" because a heart is never perfectly healed. The process of pain and healing go on in cycles. Someone might betray you, or you lose someone you love and your heart is hurt. When your heart is hurt for whatever reason, you have two choices.

1. Hide your heart behind walls and defenses you believe will protect you from ever being hurt again, which is simply not true.

OR

2. You will allow your heart to begin the healing process and keep yourself vulnerable and open to others. A defensive heart **cannot** lead other people because it is too busy running, hiding, and defending itself from the very people it is suppose to lead.

A healing heart has the power to encourage, inspire, empower, focus, challenge, influence, and increase the levels of achievement from followers. How might that affect the productivity and profitability of your business?

Check your heart, did you just read something defensively? Do you think I just said roll over and placate your followers no matter how they perform? Ask yourself, which of the following words suggest placating to you?

Encourage
Inspire
Empower
Focus
Challenge
Influence

Can you encourage someone without being misleading? Can you inspire people with power and dignity? Can you help people focus on the goal of your organization in a way that promotes ownership? Can you challenge them to give more, without threats of punishment? A leader can do all of the above in increasing measure.

There are many provisions that can help you keep your heart healing.

Real and Honest Friends

Real friends know your heart better than you. They know your weaknesses and your strengths. Ask them to give you truthful insight. Real, honest friends will tell you the truth, and not placate you.

Mentors

Mentors succeed when the student succeeds. Never let pride get in the way of receiving insight from a mentor. If you do not have a mentor, go get one. Go get several mentors. This is the fastest way to improve your leadership leverage. OPE: Other people's experience; use it wisely, use it a lot! Never reinvent the wheel when there is a mentor who can help you get ahead that much faster.

Learn from the mistakes of mentors and save yourself tons of pain. When a mentor shares a painful mistake they made, do everything in your power to feel that pain from their experience. Try to relive it in your mind, so you don't have to relive it for yourself. You do not want to go back to your mentor and say, "You were right, that didn't work."

Counselors

You may find out you have some heart issues that are not allowing you to receive wisdom from others. You might have had some extremely painful experiences in your life. Don't let your past stop you from succeeding in your future. Go to a professional and get your heart healing. You may be thinking that you are not going to a touchy-feely counselor and lay on their couch. That is an excuse to hide from your fear. You are afraid of what will be discovered. Don't be afraid; face whatever your heart is hiding and deal with it! Take courage! Overcome these obstacles and become a better leader!

Word of Warning

When seeking a professional counselor watch out for counselors who want to lower your moral expectations. Dangerous counselors think if your moral character is lowered then you won't feel bad when you break your own moral code. These pseudo counselors will challenge all the sources of your moral code and try to convince you that you are nothing more than cosmic accident with no greater goal in life than to eat, drink, and be merry for tomorrow you may die.

Find counselors that want to raise and strengthen your moral code, and give you guidance to achieve higher levels of morality. *The Golden Rule* is a moral principle. All the principles that great leaders use are moral principles. Why would you want to lower the very power that can make you greater?

The Three Tools of *The Golden Rule*

1. Self-Discipline
2. Courage
3. Empathy

You must declare war on your fears and your hurts. You must never allow past pains to mess up your present and future leadership endeavors. You must learn to pay attention to the way you are thinking and feeling in all leadership situations. You must study your thoughts and actions. This takes self-discipline. You must ask yourself, why did I say this? Why did I just do that? What was I thinking? What was I feeling?

A Powerful Question

"If I did not have to worry about the consequence of failure, how would I lead?"

Someone might state that one **does** have to worry about failure. Let me challenge you to look more closely at the question. Do you need to **worry** about failure? Those who worry plot defensively and reactively. Those who do not fret or worry about failure spend most of their time planning for success.

Powerful leadership does not think about avoiding failure. There is only one option—success! Leaders look at the prize. Don't run **from** failure, which is fundamentally defensive. Run **for** victory, which is fundamentality offensive and *way* more fun. When failure does happen it is simply a revelation, given as a gift, to point out areas that need improvement. The overall results are positive for the leader who is looking to succeed.

> Don't run from failure, which is
> ***fundamentally defensive.***
> Run for victory, which is
> ***fundamentality offensive***
> and way more fun!

Another Powerful Question

"If I did not have to worry about my followers wanting to hurt me or accuse me or want my position, how would I lead?"

This is the real question most leaders need to ask themselves. Leaders will be accused; they will be hurt and there will be people looking to rise to the top and take their job. If the leader spends precious time and energy worrying and defending the top position, like a game of king of the hill, he/she will become their own biggest threat to failure as a leader.

One cannot be self-defensive and self-protective and be considered a leader. Self-protection and leadership are diametric opposites. So pay attention to what you really worry about. Any time spent defending yourself is lost leadership. Lost leadership is the biggest threat to your job. Consequently, you may be the biggest threat to your own position.

"Do you worry?"

Worry is self-defeating

Worry steals precious time, energy, and emotions that could be used to propel your business forward. Awareness is good, but worry is bad. Worry is a destroyer of progress. Worry diminishes your leadership and depletes your business of productive energy. Worry is the mind meditating on fear. Just as empathy is a primary tool of *The Golden Rule*, worry is the primary tool used by fear. Let me encourage you to consider which one is best for your organization. As a leader do you want to worry about where your business will be in five years or do you want to dream and plan where your business will be in five years? Which choice sounds more fun and gives you greater drive?

Empathy: A Powerful Tool

Learn the discipline of empathy. Empathy is the ability to put yourself into your followers' position. Empathy is a highly refined leadership tool that empowers the leader to connect to followers in more profound and powerful ways. Empathy is a sensitive instrument that allows the leader to focus the power of *The Golden Rule* more directly. Empathy allows the leader to know what the follower needs to improve their morale, ownership, and productivity.

Steven Covey writes in his book, *The Seven Habits of Highly Effective People*, "Seek first to understand, then to be understood." That is empathy.

Leader #1. Only a selfless, confident, and courageous leader can use the tool of empathy to give people what they need to achieve greater levels of productivity.

Leader #2. A fearful leader will think,
"Who cares what the followers think, as long as they do their job."

Of the two leaders described above, who would you want to work for?

Ta-da! You just used the tool of empathy! The moment you thought about being on the receiving end you just practiced the skill of empathy.

Take a moment to put together the path of *The Golden Rule* with the information given in the preceding paragraph.

1. Use the tool of empathy to understand what is happening with a follower.

2. Develop a strategy to bring out the best of the follower. The strategy is the Correctly Applied Principle, CAP. A CAP for one follower may be different than another follower, but the goals are the same: greater morale, ownership, and productivity.

Let's consider the benefit of the simple tool of empathy in your organization. Can empathy make more money for your business? Can empathy empower your volunteers to receive criticism from you? The answer is a resounding YES!

Using empathy the leader will gain increased awareness of what the follower needs to produce more effectively. The leader can then give the follower what they need. It might be something as simple as clearer directions. A selfish leader would never see something so simple.

There might be some hard-headed (which are really hurt hearts hiding in fear) leaders out there that are thinking,

"There is no way I am going ask my employees how they are feeling all day long."

These leaders are still thinking that to understand their employees is a form of placating. Refer back to the section on placating. It is easy to forget things that we don't want to deal with.

Dealing with your heart as a leader is the most difficult challenge you will ever face. You will find yourself making excuses not to do the work. You will try to make a pseudo dichotomy of "your personal growth" and your "work" and pretend one does not affect the other. You might try to play the "martyr" as an excuse not to do the needed heart work.

"I need to lead this organization, so I will deal with my problems later. Right now, my business needs me."

That is a sad excuse not to grow as a leader. Don't fool yourself, your leadership abilities come directly from your heart. The more work you do on your heart the more effective your leadership will become and the greater the results in your organization.

With confidence and courage you
can conquer your heart!

Remove all excuses and make your heart your top priority. It will be your most fear-filled journey, but the rewards are greater than the perceived danger. Use the tools of Self-Discipline and find the Courage to proceed. Remember that principles give freedom **of** responsibility, not **from** responsibility. Be responsible and enjoy the new found freedoms of a healing heart. There are so many great achievements waiting for you.

A Leader Without A Title
Is Still A Leader!

How did you get to the position you are in now? How did you get to your current leadership position? Did you pursue higher education and were hired into a management position? Were you an entrepreneur and you started a business from scratch? Did you start at an entry level position and work your way up the corporate ladder? What if your position and your title were taken away from you? Would you still be a leader? Would you still have the ability to influence and empower people to achieve greater acts of service? Loss of title and position is the purest testing of a leader.

True leadership is what you have left when your name badge has been removed. Remove the title of President, CEO, VP, Supervisor, District Manager, Boss, and what do you have left? Have your "powers" been removed when the title and position is removed? Leadership is an issue of character.

Leadership is the ability to:
Lead people to serve other people, no matter what your label may be.

Just as exercising is good for the body, various types of service outside of your job are good for your leadership character. Consider finding a social club or organization that exists for the good of your local community. Get involved and work out your leadership character in the organization. It might be the Lions Club or Kiwanis; maybe it's time to get involved with your local church.

A true leader does not need a title to make a difference. When you find a community organization to get involved with, make sure you don't try to become the labeled leader. Do not shoot for the chair position just to obtain the title. Do your leadership from where you are. Leadership principles will work with or without the labeled position. The second most powerful principle in the universe: *The Golden Rule* will work no matter if you are a leader or not. Rest in the principles of leadership and find the unlimited courage and strength to be a leader no matter where life has you.

SECTION IV: Conclusion

There are a few final truths to guide you further as a leader. Your leadership is measurable quantitatively and qualitatively. Be your own toughest critic, but don't be your own judge and jury. Don't condemn yourself for areas of weakness or failure. If you condemn yourself for areas of weakness, you will surely do the same to your followers.

The real purpose of failure and weakness is to reveal areas that need more attention, so you can improve your leadership. Don't run or try to hide from your weaknesses and don't excuse it away claiming it is just the way you are wired. That is a fear-filled way of not being responsible for oneself. When a leader is not willing to be responsible for their whole character, they lose freedom and they lose leadership.

Understand the measurable quantitative and qualitative goal of *The Golden Rule*. The power of the second principle; *The Golden Rule*, is measurable in every area of your organization. When you use *The Golden Rule* correctly it will make you money! The Golden Rule will increase productivity! The Golden Rule will push your organization forward in ways you never dreamed possible. You already knew *The Golden Rule* from you childhood; learn to use it like an adult, and reap the rewards!

This is not a practice of touchy-feely philosophy! This is not a "feel good" philosophy either, because empathy is a tool used only by the courageous. There are many dangerous snares when you become a leader of people. Only people who courageously use empathy to CAP *The Golden Rule* become real leaders; everyone else is just pretending.

Know your true role. An unfocused understanding of your true role will lead to an unfocused organization.

A True Leader

1. You are a person
2. Who leads people
3. To serve people

1. You are a person. You are just like your followers. You are an equal to your followers in every way. The moment you begin to float above your followers, you lose your leadership ability.

2. You lead people. Your organization is made up of people. Lead the people and you will lead your business. There is no separation of business and people. They are one and the same.

3. To Serve People. From industrial corporations to personal care attendants, your organization exists to be the best at **Customer Service**; to serve people. Be the best at customer service and increase your results and profits!

The most profound truth and goal, yet the least expensive way to increase morale, productivity and profitability in your organization is **so simple**. The most cost effective way to improve you business is to know your heart.

Know Your Heart!

Correctly Apply *The Golden Rule*. Unleash the power of the second most powerful principle in the universe. You already know about the principle so why not make greater progress; why not make greater profits? The principle is free for the taking. There is no greater return on investment. *The Golden Rule* is truly golden for the Capwise leader.

Be a Capwise Leader!

Go to *capwiseleader.com* and use all the free resources provided to find and use more principles correctly. Let other leaders know what you know. Another application of *The Golden Rule* is to give good things to others. Give this book as a gift for other leaders you know. The more win/win situations you can create, the greater your leadership becomes.

Pay it Forward

Make sure all your management team is honing their correct application of *The Golden Rule*. If *The Golden Rule* is powerful for the leader, imagine the impact when your entire organization is using *The Golden Rule* effectively. Get this book into the hands of anyone who works with people whether they are a leader or a follower.

Correct Application of Principles makes you a Wise Leader!

Be a Capwise Leader!

About the Author

Jeff Rossignol; A man of principles

Jeff Rossignol is a professional speaker, author, leadership coach and entrepreneurial zealot. His entrepreneurial ventures include;

1. Capwise; Correctly Applying Principles makes a person wise.

2. Capwiseleader.com; The leadership empowerment website.

3. Deacon in his local church. Many do not consider a church as an entrepreneurial venture. A church is a non-profit volunteer-run organization. The same principles that grow any business are the same principles that will grow a church. If growing is the goal of the church, then it will take all the business savvy one can muster to effectively establish the goals of the church and CAP strategies to effectively reach the goals.

Prior to his latest ventures Jeff has served as an associate director at Bible Fellowship Church of Ephrata, Pennsylvania. He holds a masters degree in Christian Counseling. After graduate school, Jeff and his family moved to the eastern panhandle of West Virginia. Jeff has served as a vocational rehabilitation counselor for the state of West Virginia and community relations representative for Hospice of the Panhandle. Currently Jeff is serving as the marketing manager for Martinsburg Mall in West Virginia.

Ready to Move Forward?

By reading this book you have begun a new paradigm shift that will take you and your organization to new levels of success! Let me encourage you to continue your pursuit of principles with the following steps.

1. Bookmark capwiseleader.com in your web browser and use it often to expedite your CAP.

2. Contact Capwise for a free 30 minute coaching session.

3. Sign up for links to free resources, and our monthly e-zine.

Correct Application of Principles makes you a Wise Leader!

I Want to Hear From You!

I would love to hear what you think about this book! If you have any comments or suggestions about the contents of this book, or spectacular reviews about how this book helped you improve your leadership success, please take a moment to write me.
Your experience and wisdom as a leader is greatly valued!

Jeff Rossignol
Capwise
P.O. Box 261
Paw Paw, WV 25434

Jeff@capwiseleader.com

www.ingramcontent.com/pod-product-compliance
Lightning Source LLC
Chambersburg PA
CBHW021915190326
41519CB00008B/794